Diving into Pressure and Buoyancy

by:

Ron Marson, Author
Peg Marson, Illustrator

TOPS Learning Systems
342 S Plumas Street
Willows, CA 95988

www.topscience.org

Diving into Pressure and Buoyancy

Learning System: Cartesian Divers

TOPS Catalog Number: 200

Date: Feb 2008

Author: Ron Marson

Illustrator: Peg Marson

FAIR USE FEES:

• *Original Copies:* Did you purchase this download direct from TOPScience.org, or pay for a printed version? Thanks for helping us stay in business. Please enjoy using these Student Labs with the students you teach for as long as you teach!

• *Copies of Copies:* Did you receive this PDF file or a printed copy by a pathway that skipped paying TOPS? If you plan to use these materials, you owe us under the terms of our copyright. Please go to TOPScience. org, click **FAIR-USE FEE** under the "Support TOPS" menu at the left, and follow the prompts to pay **$8.50**. Or mail us a check. Your integrity helps sustain our efforts to continue delivering TOPS learning systems of the highest quality and greatest economy to teachers like you. Thanks for doing the right thing.

• *Individual Users:* Ownership of a PDF file or a printed copy of any TOPS title assigns to ONE individual (or) ONE school classroom (or) ONE family (or) ONE teaching co-op. Once ownership is assigned, it may NOT be reassigned without payment of a FAIR-USE FEE to TOPS as above. Thanks for your honesty.

• *Quantity Discounts:* Schools with multiple classrooms and teachers; school districts with multiple classrooms and teachers; co-ops with multiple user families: You may purchase 2-9 copies at a 10% discount; 10 or more copies at a 20% discount. Please calculate your FAIR-USE FEE as above. Thank you; we depend on your cooperation.

• *Workshops and Teacher Training Programs:* Please remind teachers to pay our FAIR-USE FEE if they plan to use copies of these labs in their own classrooms.

TOPS Learning Systems, 342 S Plumas Street, Willows, CA 95988 • customerservice@topscience.org • www.TOPScience.org

ISBN 978-0-941008-24-2

Diving into Pressure and Buoyancy

CONTENTS:
DIVING INTO PRESSURE AND BUOYANCY

INTRODUCTION

STUDENT LABS *and* TEACHING NOTES

STUDENT NOTES

LEARNING SYSTEM CUTOUTS

MEETING THE STANDARDS

National Science Education Standards (NRC 1996)

We have chosen to link our TOPS Labs to the national standards, even though you may have state or district-level compliance issues not addressed by the national framework. To keep our presentation relevant to local as well as national perspectives, we have fully elaborated ALL science content contained in this work, including topics not specifically named in the NRC document.

TEACHING Standards

These 14 TOPS Labs promote excellence in science teaching by these NSES criteria:
Teachers of science...
A: ...plan an inquiry-based science program. (p. 30)
B: ...guide and facilitate learning. (p. 32)
C: ...engage in ongoing assessment of their teaching and of student learning. (p. 37)
D: ...design and manage learning environments that provide students with the time, space, and resources needed for learning science. (p. 43)

CONTENT Standards

These 14 TOPS Labs contain **fundamental content** as defined by these NSES guidelines (p. 109).
• Represents a central event or phenomenon in the natural world.
• Represents a central scientific idea and organizing principle.
• Has rich explanatory power.
• Guides fruitful investigations.
• Applies to situations and contexts common to everyday experiences.
• Can be linked to meaningful learning experiences.
• Is developmentally appropriate for students at the grade level specified.

Unifying Concepts and Processes:

closed systems • open systems • regularities • theories • models • prediction • evidence • observation • explanation • interaction • change • measurement

Science as Inquiry (content standard A):

question • plan • design • investigate • gather data • classify • use technological tools • quantify • analyze • interpret • predict • communicate • reason • logic • evidence • variables • cause and effect

Physical Science (content standard B):

NSES Framework: properties of matter • changing properties • motions • forces
Core Inquiries: buoyancy • floating and sinking • pressure • Archimedes' principle • Cartesian divers • fluids • displacement • pressure changes with depth • compressibility • density • volume • temperature • weight • weightless suspension • unstable equilibrium • ideal gas relationships ($PV = kT$)
Related Explorations: air • water • Boyle's Law • Charles' Law • Newton's 3rd law (action/reaction) • cohesion/adhesion • surface tension

Science and Technology (content standard E):

invention • design • tools

GRADE LEVEL Sketches (See page 5 for grade-level adaptations.)

(K-4): Observe changes in a Cartesian diver when you squeeze this bottle. The harder you squeeze, the faster it sinks. Can you turn a packet of salsa into a Cartesian diver?

(5-8): Squeeze a bottle of water with a floating Cartesian diver sealed inside. This mechanical pressure transfers force throughout the water in all directions. Yet only compressible air inside the diver reduces to a smaller volume. Would a test object still dive if it didn't contain a compressible gas?

(9-12): Squeezing a Cartesian diver compresses its widely-spaced gas molecules much more than its closely-spaced liquid molecules. This decrease in the diver's air volume reduces the amount of water it displaces, increases its density, and decreases its buoyancy. How might you use this diver to monitor changing room temperature?

SCOPE AND SEQUENCE

CONCEPT MAP:

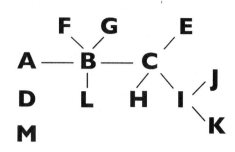

This concept map indicates that...,
- Labs **D**, **M** and **N** can stand alone.
- Labs **A**, **B**, **C** and **I** are prerequisites. Complete these before any subsequent labs joined with lines.
- Labs **F**, **G**, **L**, **E**, **H**, **J** and **K** may be completed in any order, as long as prerequisite labs are complete.

> *Use this concept map as a general sequencing guide. Adapt it further to your teaching situation with the following suggestions:*

GRADE-LEVEL ACCESSIBILILTY:

K-4: Begin with first row and extend into the second. Adapt labs as noted below for elementary access.

5-8: Begin with top three rows and extend into the fourth.

9-12: Students move independently through the concept map, choosing from all rows.

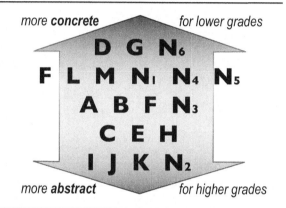

DIFFERENTIATED INSTRUCTION:

Labs A/B: These prerequisite labs develop a "Diver Catcher" tool to retrieve sunken divers without needing to empty out the 2-liter bottle and start over. Teachers who skip these labs might assemble at least one tool to use themselves, and to assist students.

C: Students with sufficient motor-skill development learn to fine-tune diver buoyancies to within just a few bubbles of air, creating positive, neutral and negative buoyancy within the same uncapped bottle of water – a prerequisite condition needed in Labs E, H, I, J, and K.

D: This lab is accessible to all grade levels, an excellent starting place for teachers short on time. Filling the dropper about ¼ full, instead of leaving it empty, makes it easier to squeeze and sink (for small hands) but harder to notice air-volume changes (for inattentive eyes).

E: This lab is accessible even to young children if teachers prepare the diver in advance. Labs A, B and C are strong prerequisites when older students build this diver for themselves.

F: Students actually feel water pressure increasing with depth! Prepare divers for younger children in advance and supervise the rubber-band pulling closely.

G: An extraordinary learning system for all ages. Prepare divers for young children in advance. Allow them ample time to manipulate, draw and write about them.

H: All ages love this competition, but subtle diver adjustments require concentrated focus plus eye-hand coordination beyond the range of younger students.

I: This prerequisite lab introduces subtle hand manipulation of open-air divers, allowing study of atmospheric pressure and temperature. Supervise closely: open plastic soda bottles make excellent water cannons!

J/K: Students with good eye-hand coordination link hover point drift (up or down), to subtle changes in pressure, temperature and volume. Use these labs to introduce higher level students to ideal gas laws: $PV = kT$.

L: Make this diver in advance for younger students. Keep the lid on and sealed tightly. If the test tube is longer than the width of the bottle that holds it, it will sink if the bottle is turned over.

M: Lower grades should skip step 3, and manipulate their condiment divers with the lids tightly sealed!

N: Watch students "catch fire" as they experience the freedom of ***being*** scientists!

TEACHING STRATEGIES

Notice that each lab page has two check-off boxes. The upper left box allows teachers to monitor completion of each lab challenge, while the lower box tracks completion of written work, which could be finished later, perhaps as homework.

This feature allows younger or less literate students to "do stuff" without necessarily having to "write stuff." If needed, you can discuss and model procedures to provide extra help for younger students.

More capable students, of course, benefit from less structure and more academic freedom. Use the table and key below to find the best balance for the students you teach. We recommend that you move down the table toward individualized learning as your students progress.

Customize TOPS to best suite your students' needs and your teaching style. Use this table and the key below!

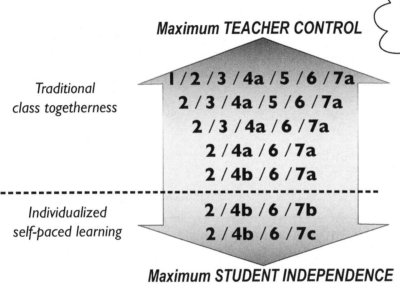

Maximum TEACHER CONTROL

Traditional class togetherness

1 / 2 / 3 / 4a / 5 / 6 / 7a
2 / 3 / 4a / 5 / 6 / 7a
2 / 3 / 4a / 6 / 7a
2 / 4a / 6 / 7a
2 / 4b / 6 / 7a

- -

Individualized self-paced learning

2 / 4b / 6 / 7b
2 / 4b / 6 / 7c

Maximum STUDENT INDEPENDENCE

STRATEGIES KEY:

1 Teacher reviews lab instructions with class.

2 Students complete lab challenge working individually or in their lab groups.

3 Teacher initials challenge check-off box.

4 Correlate key concepts in student notes to write-up questions:
   a Teacher leads a class discussion; *(or)*
   b Students read/apply notes independently.

5 Teacher models answers to at least some write-up questions.

6 Students complete response write-ups.

7 Check-off response box:
   a Teacher directs students to trade papers, correct answers, and initial; *(or)*
   b Students individually ask teacher to initial with pass / no-pass evaluation; *(or)*
   c Students maintain personal portfolio, spot-checked by teacher.

MATERIALS

This master list summarizes materials and quantities needed per student or lab group, and identifies labs that use them. To determine materials needed for specific labs, consult the "You need..." list on each student page.

QUANTITIES:

enough for one student to do all the experiments

enough for 30 students working in self-paced pairs

enough for 30 students working in pairs, all doing the same lesson

LABS:	n/n/n	ITEM:
most labs	1/15/15	2-liter plastic soda bottles with tight-fitting lids (clean, labels removed)
most labs	1/1/1	water
most labs	1/15/15	glass eyedroppers, available from TOPS (see Notes A1 for specifications)
A, B	.5/8/8	feet waxed dental floss
some labs	1/2/8	scissors
A, N2, N4	3/17/20	straight plastic straws (avoid very wide ones)
some labs	1/15/15	towels, rags, or sponges to wipe up spills
B	1/2/4	paper punch tools
F, G	1.1/17/17	meters string (heavier than kite string and lighter than cord)
F, G	3/30/45	craft sticks or tongue depressors
F	1/5/15	thick rubber bands (not likely to break when pulled hard)
E, N4	1/5/15	thin rubber bands
J	1/15/15	inches clear tape
K	1/1/1	access to cool water (from a tap or a refrigerator)
L	1/8/15	test tubes
L, M	1/5/15	deep glasses or tall jars
I, L	1/5/15	tubs or trays to catch water overflow
M	1/7/15	condiment packets (fast-food type) that float in water
M	1/5/15	paper clips
M, N4	1/15/15	pinches modeling clay (oil-based, waterproof)
N2	1/15/15	staples
N5	1/2/8	boxes of paper clips

GETTING READY

☐ **Review Scope and Sequence** (p 5) to understand which labs best apply to the grade level you teach. Then read questions posed in bold at the top of these labs (pp 9-22) to gain an overall sense of the experimental challenges that will best engage your students. Finally, decide how many labs your students have time to investigate, budgeting, on average, a class period for each one they might complete.

☐ **Photocopy Student Labs** you decide to use. These may be just a few, or the complete set A-N. Fold back the teaching notes at the bottom of each page so only the labs appear at the top of your copies, with blank space underneath.

• To produce <u>consumable</u> worksheets: copy one lab per student, then direct students to organize their written responses in the white space below each lab.

• To produce <u>nonconsumable</u> reference pages: copy, collate and staple sets of lab instructions, one per lab group. Lab groups in different periods throughout the school day reference these same instructions, organizing written work and receiving checkpoints on their own notebook paper.

• Please observe our copyright restrictions. Our intention is for each purchaser to have unlimited personal use. Our need is for educators not share or trade lessons without compensating TOPS.

☐ **Photocopy Students Notes** (pp 23-26). These explain the key concepts, condensed into direct, simple language, needed to understand the labs and answer the response questions.

• If your students are capable of independent study and inquiry, we recommend that you photocopy a set of these notes for each student. These notes, together with labs instructions and access to simple materials, provide everything they need to become their own best science investigators.

• If your students are not yet capable of independent study and inquiry, keep leading them toward independence. In the meantime, reference these original pages to teach key concepts and facilitate class discussion. You'll need no extra copies, unless you wish to distribute study notes.

☐ **Photocopy learning system cutouts.** (p 26). These are needed only for upper level students who complete Labs J and K.

☐ **Organize a way to track assignments.** It may be a good idea to keep student work on file in class. If you lack file space, substitute an empty copy paper box and a brick. File folders and notebooks both make suitable organizers. A sheet of notebook paper taped inside the front cover can list which labs are completed and which are in progress. Students will feel a sense of accomplishment as their papers accumulate into an impressive portfolio. Reference and review are facilitated because all assignments stay together in one place.

☐ **Collect needed materials** (page 7).

☐ **Observe safety precautions.**

• Wet floors can be slippery. Keep mop, towels or sponges available to quickly wipe up spills.

• Labs I, J and K involve open-air divers. Students who squeeze them, forgetting the lid is off, produce unanticipated fountains.

• Lab F involves pulling back on a rubber band with considerable force. Degraded, damaged or thin bands could break and inflict a painful snap.

• Labs L and N5 use glass test tubes. Breakage is possible, so supervise closely.

• Since it is impossible to anticipate every situation that could arise, TOPS Learning Systems can not be held liable for misuse of these materials or lack of appropriate supervision. Users agree that students and teachers must accept personal responsibility to exercise reasonable care.

☐ **Communicate your grading expectations.** We recommend that you grade on individual effort, attitude and overall achievement:

• Effort: How many labs and how much written work has the student completed? Of what quality?

• Attitude: Has the student worked to capacity, or wasted time? What evidence of personal initiative and responsibility?

• Achievement: Assign tasks or ask questions that assess how well students have mastered key concepts.

Challenge: *Can you rescue an eyedropper "diver" from the bottom of a bottle?*

You need: a 2-liter plastic soda bottle, water, an eyedropper, waxed dental floss, scissors, 2 narrow plastic soda straws, a towel or rag to wipe up spills.

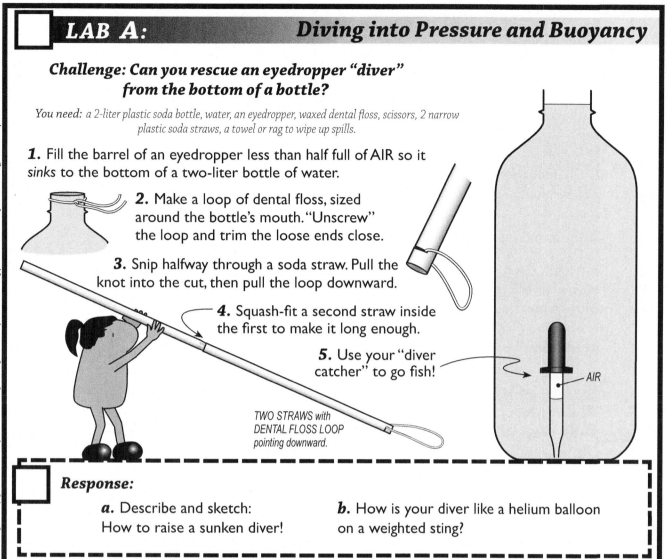

1. Fill the barrel of an eyedropper less than half full of AIR so it *sinks* to the bottom of a two-liter bottle of water.

2. Make a loop of dental floss, sized around the bottle's mouth. "Unscrew" the loop and trim the loose ends close.

3. Snip halfway through a soda straw. Pull the knot into the cut, then pull the loop downward.

4. Squash-fit a second straw inside the first to make it long enough.

5. Use your "diver catcher" to go fish!

TWO STRAWS with DENTAL FLOSS LOOP pointing downward.

AIR

Response:

a. Describe and sketch: How to raise a sunken diver!

b. How is your diver like a helium balloon on a weighted sting?

TEACHING NOTES

Learning Objective

To improvise a "catcher" with which to rescue an eyedropper "diver" from a bottle of water. To practice rescue skills.

Lab Notes

1. Eyedroppers must be glass (not plastic), with air-tight rubber bulbs. Pull off the plastic screw-on cap, if any. Ideally, this eyedropper should sink with just one "intake" (squeeze-and-release) of water. Droppers requiring more than one "intake" of water must (inconveniently) be upended and tapped, so more air rises to the tip, which can then be squeezed out to allow more water to be sucked in.

5. Direct the floss almost straight downward in an open loop to start. The water will buoy it upward, roughly perpendicular to the straw, ideal for looping over the diver's collar.

Challenge Check-Off

Students should demonstrate an ability to retrieve the dropper from the bottom of the bottle, without pouring out the water.

Response Check-Off

a. Students should sketch their "diver catcher" as illustrated above, and label its parts, then describe how to raise the diver: lower the floss loop below the rim of the rubber bulb, then pull upward so this loop catches under the bulb's rim.

b. The air-filled rubber bulb corresponds to the balloon; the heavy glass barrel to the weight at the end of the string. Just as heavier air buoys up the helium-filled balloon, even so, heavier water buoys up the air-filled bulb.

Test for Understanding

Which end of your "standing" diver displaces (pushes away) more water, the top or the bottom? Why?

The top of the diver displaces more water because it is filled with air. This air prevents water from moving higher up the tube and entering the rubber bulb. *Water inside the glass tube no longer weighs down the diver as it did in air! This "inside" water joins the "outside" water it is immersed in, to become one medium. It is now weightless in the sense that it is supported by the self-same weight of the water it displaces.*

LAB B: Diving into Pressure and Buoyancy

Challenge: Can you pick a floating Diver from the mouth of a bottle?

You need: the diver catcher from Lab A, a paper punch, a plastic soda bottle full of water, an eyedropper, a towel.

1. Fill the barrel of an eyedropper a little more than half full of AIR so it floats in the mouth of your bottle.

2. Try to pick up the floating diver with your fingers.

3. Notch the free end of your diver catcher with a paper punch to help you pick up the diver.

pinch flat and use
HOLE PUNCH

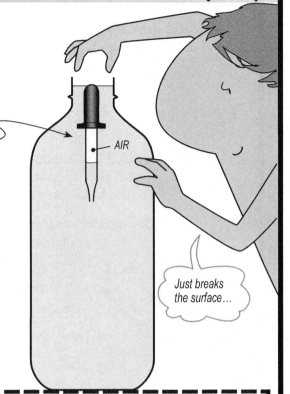

AIR

Just breaks the surface...

---

a. Describe and sketch: How to grab a floating diver.

b. Why does your diver now float, when it sank in Lab A? What *variable* did you change?

c. Could a tiny water bug swim into the dropper from the outside? Explain.

TEACHING NOTES

Learning Objective

To complete construction of the diver catcher. To practice "grabbing" a low-floating diver from the mouth of a bottle of water.

Challenge Check-Off

Students should demonstrate an ability to lift a low-floating dropper from the mouth of the bottle using the notched end of their diver catcher.

Lab Notes

2. It is not possible to finger-pick a low-floating diver.

Response Check-Off

a. Students should sketch the notched end of their diver catcher and describe its use: Place this notch over the dropper's rubber "collar" and lift upward. Press sideways while lifting to prevent the collar from slipping out of the notch.

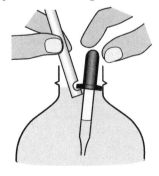

b. Air volume is the significant variable that has changed. The diver now floats because it holds more air. *It thereby displaces more water, which increases its buoyancy.*

c. Yes. A tiny water bug could swim in and out of the dropper without restriction. Water outside the dropper is not separated from water inside. *This question helps students understand that "inside water," like "outside water," is all part of the "sea" the diver floats in. "Inside water" does not weigh the diver down unless beads of water cling above the waterline inside the dropper.*

Test For Understanding

• Did your diver float because (a) you added less water, or (b) you added more air? Explain.

The diver floats because (b) I added more air. This larger volume of air displaces a larger volume of water, thereby increasing the diver's buoyancy.

Why not (a)? Adding less water to the dropper makes it weigh less in air, yet it floats, weightless, in water. Once immersed, its "inside" and "outside" water merge into one body that supports the floating diver. It is not weighed down by "inside" water, unless separate droplets have splashed into the air-filled chamber.

LAB C: Diving into Pressure and Buoyancy

Challenge: Can the same diver both sink and swim?

You need: the diver catcher developed in Labs A and B,
a soda bottle full of water, an eyedropper, a towel.

1. Fill an eyedropper diver with *just* enough air
to *barely float* at the mouth of your bottle.

2. Test if your diver stays sunk when pushed to
the bottom with your diver catcher. (If it refloats,
add slightly more water.)

3. Nudge your diver up and down with your
diver catcher. Show that it both sinks and floats
without subtracting or adding any air!

a. Explain how to fine-tune your diver, giving
it slightly more or less air volume.

b. Is it possible to change the volume of air
inside a diver without adding or removing air?
Propose your best hypothesis.

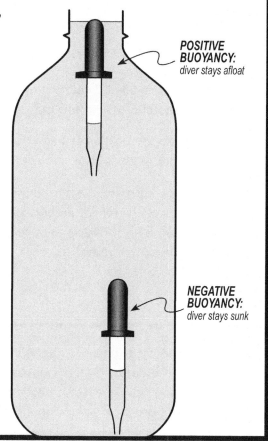

POSITIVE BUOYANCY:
diver stays afloat

NEGATIVE BUOYANCY:
diver stays sunk

TEACHING NOTES

Learning Objective

To adjust the volume of air in an eyedropper so it has
positive buoyancy at the top of a bottle of water, and negative buoyancy at the bottom. To propose an hypothesis to
account for this phenomenon.

Lab Notes

1-2. Through trial-and-error adjustment, students should
fill the dropper with just enough air so the rubber bulb
barely breaks the surface. *Remind students that they add or
subtract air (not water), to increase or decrease buoyancy. They
accomplish this, of course, by working with water.*

Challenge Check-Off

Students should demonstrate that the diver stays sunk
when pushed down, and stays afloat when "looped" or
"notch-nudged" back to the surface. *Ask how the diver's
buoyancy could possibly change when you neither added nor
subtracted air!*

Response Check-Off

a. To increase buoyancy, **add air.** (Take the dropper out of the
water, then squeeze out a little water to allow in a little air.)

To decrease buoyancy, **subtract air.** (Holding the tip of the
dropper under water, squeeze out all the water, plus an additional bubble of air. Relaxing the bulb will then allow in all
the expelled water, plus one more drop to replace the expelled
air bubble.)

b. Yes. Water pressure increases with depth. The diver is under
greater *pressure* at the bottom of the bottle than at the top,
because more water is pressing on it from above. This compresses the air inside to a slightly smaller volume, even though
all of the original air remains inside. *Let all theories stand, for
now, without correction. Lab D will make this expansion and con-
traction of air due to pressure much more obvious.*

Test for Understanding

How do you know that water pressure or air pressure increases with depth? What evidence can you cite?

• *My eyedropper's buoyancy changes from positive to negative with
increasing water depth.*

• *My ears feel the pressure when I dive to the bottom of a pool, or
drive down a mountain pass, deeper into Earth's "ocean" of air.*

LAB D: Diving into Pressure and Buoyancy

Challenge: Can you sink a diver completely filled with air?

You need: an eyedropper, a plastic soda bottle full of water plus the cap.

1. Float an air-filled ("empty") eyedropper in a bottle full of water and cap tightly.

2. Squeeze the bottle hard and observe! (You've just made a *Cartesian Diver*.)

3. Can you squeeze just hard enough so your diver "hovers" (neither floats nor sinks)? By how much does the air volume shrink inside?

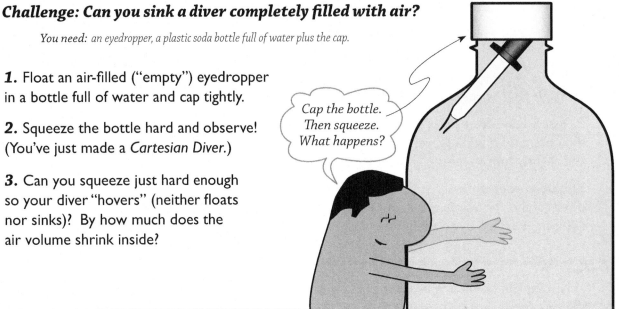

Cap the bottle. Then squeeze. What happens?

a. What happens to the empty diver when you squeeze the bottle?

b. Why does squeezing the bottle push water up inside the diver?

c. When does your diver have negative buoyancy? Neural buoyancy? Positive buoyancy?

d. Evaluate your hypothesis in Lab C (if you completed that lab).

TEACHING NOTES

Learning Objective

To observe the floating and sinking properties of a Cartesian Diver. To experience the relationship between air volume and pressure.

Lab Notes

1. Wonder aloud: The dropper was 100% full of air before you placed it in the water bottle and tightened the lid. Now water has already pushed up into its tip (as illustrated above).

2. Students with small hands, or less gripping strength, might place the bottle against a wall, and push on one side.

The Cartesian Diver was so named in honor of the French philosopher Rene Descartes. Historically there is no evidence that he ever experimented with buoyancy in this manner.

Challenge Check-Off

Students should demonstrate an ability to make the diver rise, fall and hover by squeezing the bottle with varying force. They should interpret the water level inside the glass barrel as an indication of the diver's air volume that compresses and expands with more or less applied pressure.

Response Check-Off

a. When I squeezed the bottle, water rose into the diver, which first swung into a vertical floating position, then sank as I pressed harder. When I stopped squeezing, water rushed back out of the dropper, and it rose again to the surface.

b. Squeezing the bottle forces water inside. Air in the diver (a compressible gas) gets squeezed into a smaller volume by water (a non-compressible liquid) entering the barrel.

c. The diver has negative buoyancy when it sinks under high pressure. It has neutral buoyancy when it hovers under medium pressure. It has positive buoyancy when it floats under low pressure.

d. The diver remains sunk at the bottom in lab C because its air was compressed under the weight of more water. Water pressure increases with depth.

Test For Understanding

The diver is completely filled with air. Yet water enters the tip of the tube. What's going on? *Air inside the dropper is being compressed by the depth of the water and the pressure exerted by tightly screwing on the lid.*

Going Further

• Can you adjust your diver so it sinks and floats with a very gentle squeeze?

Displace some of its air with water to make the diver less buoyant. (In labs that follow, students will have many other opportunities like this to fine tune the buoyancy of their divers.)

LAB E: Diving into Pressure and Buoyancy

Challenge: Can you launch a rocket diver?

You need: diver-tuning skills taught in lab C, materials to make a Cartesian diver (bottle, cap, eyedropper, and water), a diver catcher, a towel.

1. Adjust the buoyancy of your Cartesian diver so it:

- Dives to the bottom with a *gentle* squeeze, and…
- Remains on the bottom, and…
- Rockets back to the surface with a *hard* squeeze and quick release!

2. Use a thin rubber band to mark the depth at which this rocket diver hovers weightless inside your bottle. (Slide the rubber band into the same plane as the diver's collar.)

Hover point!

---

a. Sketch a large picture of your bottle and rubber band.
  - Draw 3 divers in these positions: sunk, hovering, floating.
  - Which diver displaces (exactly / less than / more than) its own weight in water?

b. Why does a quick release of the bottle make the diver rocket upward?

TEACHING NOTES

Learning Objective

To understand buoyancy in terms of Archimedes' Principle. To understand rocket thrust in terms of Newton's Third Law of action and reaction.

Lab Notes

1. Students must adjust air volumes in their droppers (as in Lab C), so they both float at the top and sink at the bottom, then screw on the lid (unlike Lab C).

Challenge Check-Off

Students should demonstrate that their Cartesian diver floats at the surface, remains sunk at the bottom, and rockets past neutral buoyancy defined by a rubber band (when squeezed and quickly released).

Response Check-Off

a. *Differences in water displacement are exaggerated for clarity.*

The hovering diver displaces exactly its own weight in water. The floating diver displaces more than its own

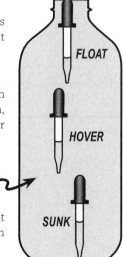

FLOAT

HOVER

SUNK

weight in water, the sunken diver displaces less than its own weight.

b. Quickly releasing pressure on the bottle causes air in the diver to rapidly expand, propelling the water downward, out of the dropper. As this mass of water is forced downward, the diver is pushed upward with an equal and opposite force. *Newton's third law, from the Student Notes page.*

Test for Understanding

Must you maintain continuous rocket thrust to raise the diver to the surface of the water? Explain.

No. Rocket thrust is only required to carry the diver beyond the rubber band. Once the diver has risen above neutral buoyancy, positive buoyancy will continue to lift it to the surface.

LAB F: Diving into Pressure and Buoyancy

Challenge: Can you make your diver hover weightless at all water depths?

You need: a Cartesian diver, a diver catcher, heavy string, scissors, a craft stick or tongue depressor, a heavy rubber band, a towel.

1. Adjust your Cartesian diver so it dives with easy squeezes, yet always rises and floats again.

2. Wrap heavy string 3 times around the bottle, like a belt. Borrow someone's finger to help tie it off *tightly* with a double knot.

3. Insert a flat stick, with a thick rubber band over the top, into the belt as shown.

4. Pull the rubber band to compress air in your diver. (Brace the bottle with your thumb above the stick.)

- The harder you pull the rubber band, the more pressure you place on the diver.

- Your diver hovers when its average density equals the density of water (1 g/mL). This only happens when you keep the diver under constant pressure.

Notice how much "stretch" you use to control the diver at different depths.

a. Explain how to make your diver descend *very* slowly, and hover at will.

b. If the diver hovers only at one constant density and pressure, why must you keep changing tension on the rubber band to make it hover higher or lower?

TEACHING NOTES

Learning Objective

To develop a kinesthetic feel for how water pressure increases with depth. To understand that a diver hovers in weightless buoyancy when its average density equals the density of water.

Lab Notes

1. In other words, the diver has positive buoyancy at all bottle depths.

2-3. The easiest way to position the rubber band is to place it over the end of the craft stick *before* sliding the stick under the belt, then adjusting as shown.

3-4. Use a thick rubber band that won't break and inflict a painful snap. Recycled produce bands, like those on broccoli, are suitable. (Or substitute a loop of heavy string. Unfortunately, this eliminates the dramatic stretch variations that so clearly show changing water-depth pressures.)

The *density* of water is 1 g/mL at all water depths, because liquids are essentially incompressible. Air density, by contrast, changes dramatically with depth because air is a gas. Air compressibility demands ever-changing rubber-band tension to keep the diver hovering under constant pressure and density (1 g/mL).

Challenge Check-Off

Students should demonstrate slow, controlled diver descents and ascents, stopping to hover at any depth along the way.

Response Check-Off

a. Pull the rubber band tightly so the diver just begins to sink. Maintain high tension so the diver hovers just under the surface. Increase the tension to begin a further descent, then gradually ease the tension to make the dive as slow as you like. Hovering near the bottom requires only light tension.

b. Water pressure increases with depth. By gradually easing the rubber band as the diver dives, you balance *increasing* pressure on the diver due to water depth with *decreasing* pressure due to rubber band tension, thus maintaining a constant hover pressure and hover density (1 g/mL).

Test for Understanding

Why does your Cartesian diver hover under high rubber-band tension at the top of the bottle, and hover under low rubber-band tension at the bottom?

This compensates for low pressure at the top of the bottle and high pressure at the bottom due to increased water depth. This trade-off keeps air pressures inside the diver constant. A bug riding inside the glass barrel above waterline would sense no pressure change.

LAB G: Diving into Pressure and Buoyancy

Challenge: Can you make your Diver hover weightless, without touching the bottle?

You need: a Cartesian diver with string belt from Lab F, a craft stick or tongue depressor, a round pen or pencil.

1. Get your diver with triple-string belt from Lab F. (Remove the rubber band.)

2. Insert a flat stick under the belt, and a round pen or pencil under the stick as shown.

3. Keeping both hands on the pen, can you make the diver's "collar" hover at belt-level?

4. Keeping this pressure setting, can you make your diver hover *above* belt line by touching *only* the cap?

5. Can you make your diver hover for one minute without touching anything at all?

Slide or roll a pen or pencil higher or lower to control pressure.

a. How do you control the motion of your diver with the pen?

b. What happens to each of these diver variables as you roll the pen downward: pressure, volume, density, water displacement, and buoyancy.

c. Assume your diver hovers at the belt-line. Describe regions of positive, negative and neutral buoyancy within the bottle.

TEACHING NOTES

Learning Objective

To use subtle pressure changes to control a diver that has neutral buoyancy. To discover that a diver's hover point is inherently unstable.

Lab Notes

1. Or complete Lab F, steps 1 and 2.

2-3. Roll the pen downward to lever the stick against the bottle and thus increase pressure on the diver. To exert additional pressure, insert two (or more) craft sticks and roll the pen between them.

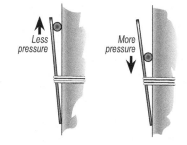

Less pressure

More pressure

Challenge Check-Off

(3) Keeping both hands on the pen, students should roll it up or down (in the same direction they want the diver to move), until the diver's collar hovers approximately at belt level. (4) At this pressure setting, they can control the diver simply by pressing the cap, more and more lightly as the diver's collar approaches the belt line. (5) No matter how finely they adjust the

hover point, however, the diver will soon drift into positive or negative buoyancy, and "fall" up or down.

Response Check-Off

a. Roll the pen up or down, in the same direction you want your diver to move.

b. Roll the pen down: This increases water pressure on the diver, shrinks the air inside the diver to a smaller volume, increases the diver's average density, causes it to displace less water, decreases its buoyancy, makes it sink.

c. The belt-line defines a plane a neutral buoyancy within the bottle. Moving higher than "belt-plane" the diver acquires increasingly positive buoyancy and floats. Moving lower than "belt-plane" the diver acquires increasingly negative buoyancy and sinks.

Test for Understanding

You know that water pressure increases with depth. Why does this make your diver's hover position unstable?

The slightest down-drift increases pressure on the diver to make it "fall downward" faster and faster. The slightest up-drift decreases pressure on the diver to make it "fall upward" faster and faster.

LAB H: Diving into Pressure and Buoyancy

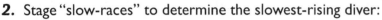

Challenge: Who can fine-tune their diver to rise the slowest?

Ready,... set,...

You need: a Cartesian diver, a towel, a diver catcher, a towel.

1. Adjust the air in your diver so it has near-neutral buoyancy at the bottom of the bottle, with just enough lift to rise back to the surface:
 • Always test your diver with the lid on.
 • When you screw-on the lid, hold the inflexible neck, never the flexible sides.

2. Stage "slow-races" to determine the slowest-rising diver:
 • **Last** diver to bump the bottle cap wins.
 • No fair re-tuning your diver once competition begins.
 • Divers that fail to launch are disqualified.

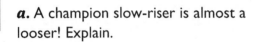

a. A champion slow-riser is almost a looser! Explain.

b. Why does a diver accelerate (rise faster and faster), as it floats to the surface?

TEACHING NOTES

Learning Objective

To finely adjust air volumes in a Cartesian diver. To win a "slowest-rising-diver" competition.

Lab Notes

1. Tightening the lid while holding onto the inflexible neck, slightly increases bottle pressure (slightly reducing diver buoyancy), in a predictable way. Tightening the lid while holding onto the flexible sides, however, may inadvertently squeeze air out of the bottle just before sealing. This dramatically lowers bottle pressure, (increasing diver buoyancy), in unpredictable ways.

2. You can *subtract* air, one bubble at a time, by holding the tip of the dropper under water. Squeeze out all water, plus one bubble of air, before relaxing the bulb to again draw in water.

You can *add* tiny increments of air to the diver by wiping the wet dropper tip with dry fingers.

Less water, more air

Challenge Check-Off

Any number of competitors can bring their divers together to race. Clever students might tilt their bottles

while squeezing them down to the "starting line." This allows their diver to begin its ascent near the side, possibly dragging itself along the inside surface as it creeps to the top.

Response Check-Off

a. The slightest increase in the air volume of a diver that *just* fails to launch could make it a slow-rising champion. There is negligible difference between disqualification and becoming the slowest rising diver.

b. Water pressure increases with depth. As a diver rises, it is submerged under less and less water, and thus subjected to less and less pressure. This allows air trapped inside the diver to continually expand, and thus buoy it up with ever increasing force.

Test for Understanding

Assume you have fine-tuned a champion slow-rising diver. Would you expect it to perform equally in a shorter bottle? A taller bottle?

A champion slow-rising diver is fine tuned to a specific depth of water. It would launch and rise faster in a shorter bottle with less water pressure due to depth. It would fail to launch in a taller bottle with more water pressure due to depth.

LAB I: Diving into Pressure and Buoyancy

Challenge: Can you control an open diver with your bare hands?

You need: a Cartesian diver, a diver catcher, a tub or tray to catch water overflow, a towel, a thin rubber band.

1. Lower water in your diver bottle to the base of the neck. Place it on a towel to absorb spills.

2. Get your Diver Catcher. Add or subtract air, so your diver *both* sinks and floats in an *open* bottle of water (no lid).

3. Can you make your floating diver **sink**, using two hands?

4. Can you make your sunken diver **float**, using two hands?

5. Can you make your diver **hover**, using just *one* hand?

6. Mark where your open-air diver hovers without external hand pressure. (Line up a thin rubber band on the bottle in the same plane as the hovering diver's collar.)

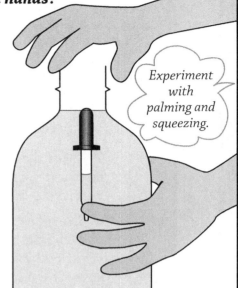

Experiment with palming and squeezing.

a. Describe how you pressured your diver to sink, float and hover in an open bottle of water.

b. Describe how to locate your open-air diver's hover point.

TEACHING NOTES

Learning Objective

To discover, develop and refine ways to apply hand pressure to an open bottle of water to make a diver sink, float, and hover.

Lab Notes

1. Students might remove water with their eye dropper, or simply pour it out. The water level should not fall below the straight neck. Otherwise the floating diver becomes more difficult to catch with the notched Diver Catcher.

2. Students did this previously in Lab C. This create 3 states of buoyancy in the bottle: positive above, negative below, with neutral somewhere in between.

3-6. These challenges, at first, may not seem possible. So allow plenty of discovery time. Supervise students closely to minimize water spills and horseplay. Store open-air divers, when not in use, with lids on.

Challenge Check-Off

Students should demonstrate an ability to make their open-air divers: (3) sink by palm-capping, then side-squeezing; (4) float by side-squeezing, then palm capping; (5) hover anywhere above the rubber band by applying variable pressure to the bottle's mouth with the palm of one hand; (6) hover momentarily at rubber band level without applying hand pressure.

Response Check-Off

a. To *sink* the diver: Cap the bottle's mouth with the palm of one hand, then squeeze the bottle with the other hand to increase pressure on the diver and decrease its buoyancy.

To *float* the diver: Gently squeeze water higher in the bottle, then cap with the other hand. Water will sink back into a slightly collapsed bottle, decreasing pressure on the diver and increasing its buoyancy. *The collapsing weight of the water expands trapped air inside both bottle and diver, creating "negative pressure" somewhat lower than outside atmospheric pressure.*

To make the diver *hover*: Press the mouth of the bottle with one palm as the diver floats at the surface, and it will begin to sink. Press more lightly and you can make the diver hover in a state of neutral buoyancy, displacing exactly its own weight in water, so it has the same density as water.

b. Press a palm on the bottle's mouth with a diver floating inside. As the diver begins to sink, ease the pressure. You will discover a depth at which the diver hovers under the pressure of air and water depth alone, without hand pressure. This is the diver's "hover point." Mark it (at the diver's collar level) with a rubber band.

Test for Understanding

An open-air diver hovers at rubber-band level, without any externally applied hand pressure. Is this diver still under pressure?

Yes. It is under the weight of Earth's atmosphere pressing on the bottle of water in all directions, and the weight of the water pressing on the dropper in all directions.

LAB J: Diving into Pressure and Buoyancy

Challenge: Does a diver's hover point change when you cap the bottle?

You need: experience with lab I, a Cartesian diver, a diver catcher, a towel, scissors, a Centimeter Ruler cutout, clear tape.

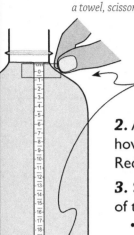

1. Cut out the Centimeter Ruler. Tape it vertically to the neck and body of your bottle as shown, zero end up.

2. Adjust the air in your diver so it hovers in this bottle *without* a lid. Record the depth at collar level.

3. Screw on the lid. (Hold the neck of the bottle, not the sides.)
 • Hypothesize: Will your diver hover at the same depth as before?
 • Observations?
 • Conclusion?

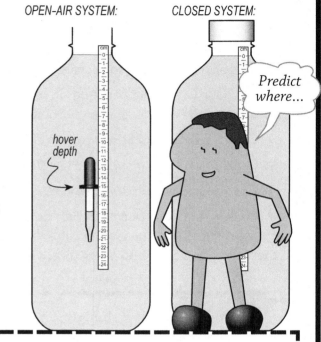

OPEN-AIR SYSTEM:

CLOSED SYSTEM:

Predict where...

hover depth

a. Write up steps 2 and 3.

b. How might your *open-air* diver respond to a sudden drop in barometric (air) pressure caused by an approaching storm?

TEACHING NOTES

Learning Objective

To correlate relative up and down changes in a diver's hover point with changes in pressure.

Lab Notes

2. Encourage students to approach the diver's hover point from above (never below). That is, starting with a floating diver, they should palm the mouth of the bottle with less and less pressure until it floats weightless, at atmospheric pressure. If it sinks, begin again from the top See Lab Notes K.

Challenge Check-Off

Students should demonstrate an ability to make their divers hover and record the corresponding hover point with and without the bottle lid in place.

As opportunities arise, ask students to verbalize their hypotheses and/or conclusions. Will/did screwing down the lid change the hover point?

Response Check-Off

a. Hypothesis: Capping the bottle will place the diver under higher pressure, and raise its hover point. *Previously, the diver hovered higher in the bottle with more palm pressure applied, and lower with less (or no) palm pressure.*

Observations: Expect the hover point to rise a few or many centimeters, depending on (1) the lid's fit, (2) how tightly it was screwed on while holding the inflexible bottle neck. Large pressure increases may raise the final hover point "above the top," making the diver negatively buoyant at all bottle depths. *If air was inadvertently squeezed out by holding (and squeezing) the flexible middle while the lid was being closed, LOWER pressures could be created inside the bottle which would subsequently drive the hover point lower, possibly "through the floor," making the diver positively buoyant at all bottle depths.*

Conclusion: Increasing pressure raises the hover point. *And decreasing pressure lowers the hover point.*

b. A sudden drop in barometric pressure should lower the hover point. Decreasing pressure allows air to expand in the diver and increase its buoyancy. To hover again, therefore, the diver would need to sink under more water to shrink its air volume back to previous size and once again float weightless, at the same average density as the density of water.

Test for Understanding

How could you use an open-air Cartesian diver to predict changes in weather? *Monitor its hover point. A rising hover point indicates higher atmospheric pressure and fair weather. A falling hover point indicates lower atmospheric pressure and foul weather. (Since temperature is another variable that matters, this diver would have to be maintained at constant temperature.)*

LAB K: *Diving into Pressure and Buoyancy*

Challenge: *Is your diver a temperature sensor?*

You need: A Cartesian diver with a centimeter depth ruler (from Lab J), a diver catcher, cold tap water (or overnight chilling in a refrigerator).

1. Get your Cartesian diver with centimeter ruler still attached.

2. Refill the bottle with cold water (or bring it chilled from a refrigerator). Remove the lid for this lab.

3. Adjust the air in your eyedropper so it floats at the top and stays sunk at the bottom.

4. Find out where your diver hovers. Descend *from the surface* by palming the open mouth of the bottle.

5. How do you think your diver's hover point will change as the water warms?

- Make a prediction.
- Take hover readings every 5 minutes or so, and make a data table.

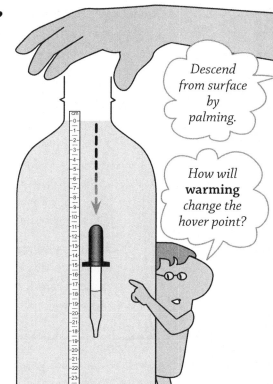

Descend from surface by palming.

*How will **warming** change the hover point?*

---

a. Report your prediction and conclusions.

b. How is your diver like a "backwards" thermometer?

TEACHING NOTES

Learning Objective

To correlate relative up and down changes in a diver's hover point with changes in temperature.

Lab Notes

4. The difference between top-down hover point readings and bottom-up readings can amount to several centimeters. This is because the meniscus (the water's curved surface inside the dropper) tends to move in abrupt jumps rather than slide smoothly. The meniscus in a descending diver is likely to be "stuck" at a somewhat greater air volume, and a rising diver is likely to be stuck at a somewhat smaller air volume, as it approaches the hover point. Students can control for this "sticky adhesion" variable by always taking hover point readings on a *descending* diver.

5. When the hover point drops to the bottom of the bottle, so the diver is positively buoyant at all levels, advise students to expel air and continue taking readings. *Each air bubble expelled allows the diver to hover perhaps 6 cm higher.*

Challenge Check-Off

Students should record a data table that demonstrates a down-trending hover point as the cold water warms over time. Ask students why they think this is happening. *See Prediction (a), below.*

Response Check-Off

a. Prediction: Warming water expands the air in the dropper. This causes it to displace more water and increase its buoyancy. This extra buoyancy allows it to hover lower, under greater water pressure, before sinking to the bottom.

Conclusion: The hover point drifts downward as temperature increases. *Depending on temperature differences between cool bottle water and warm room air, expect the warming, expanding air inside the diver to lower its hover depth, by roughly 1/2 centimeter per minute.*

b. The diver's hover point moves in a direction opposite a thermometer. It goes down when the temperature goes up, and goes up when the temperature goes down.

Test for Understanding

You want a diver to signal you when your room begins to cool. Would you set it to barely stay floating at the top of the bottle, or to barely stay sunk on the bottom? *Set it to barely float. When the room cools, it will raise the hover point above the diver, thereby sinking it with negative buoyancy.*

LAB L: Diving into Pressure and Buoyancy

Challenge: Can you turn a test tube into a diver?

You need: A bottle of water with lid, a test tube, a container of water taller than your test tube, an eye dropper, a towel, a tub or tray to catch water overflow, a diver catcher.

FLIP TEST TUBE **QUICKLY** *INTO BOTTLE*

1. Add water to a test tube to float it, mouth up, within about 2 millimeters of sinking.

2. Hold the test tube next to a bottle brim full of water, and up-end it into the bottle. Be quick so water can't fall out of the test tube.

3. Have you made a Cartesian diver? Can you operate it with and without a lid?

Start with the bottle brimming over.

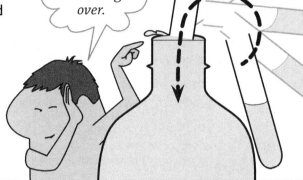

a. Explain how to make your inverted test tube dive and resurface. Include these terms in your answer: pressure, volume, density, water displacement and buoyancy.

b. How would you make your diver more sensitive to changes in pressure?

TEACHING NOTES

Learning Objective

To turn a test tube into a Cartesian diver. To understand why it floats and sinks.

Lab Notes

1. This brings the test tube to near-neutral buoyancy. *Students might avoid repeating this step by marking this water level in the test tube with a small rubber band.*

2. This operation is easier than it looks if you start with the two mouths close together. A quick twist of the wrist inverts the tube over the bottle. Centrifugal force helps keep water from falling out so that no extra air gets in.

Challenge Check-Off

Students should demonstrate that they can make their inverted test tube dive and rise with the lid on, then off.

Response Check-Off

a. To make the inverted test tube dive, squeeze a capped bottle, or press palm down on an open-mouthed bottle with no lid. This increases water pressure on the air inside the test tube; shrinks it to a smaller volume; increases the diver's average density; causes it to displace less water; decreases its

buoyancy; makes it sink. Releasing the pressure affects all of these variables in reverse.

b. With the test tube right-side-up, add a little more water so it floats a little closer to the water line. This will displace slightly more air when it is inverted so that it will float closer to neutral buoyancy.

Test for Understanding

As a swimmer, how can you adjust your body to neutral buoyancy? *I'll empty air from my lungs (displace less water), until I barely break the surface of the water, then I'll breathe out slightly more air. My body weight now equals the weight of the water I displace, so I hover in weightless suspension. My body has the same average density as the water that surrounds me.*

Going Further

Can you make a floating inverted test tube hover by adding or subtracting mass with straight pins in a rubber band?

How does added mass affect the diver's hover point? *It hovers higher.*

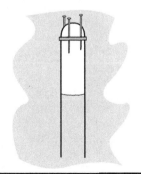

LAB M: Diving into Pressure and Buoyancy

Lab M: Can you turn a fast-food condiment packet into an open-air diver?

You need: a bottle of water, a condiment packet that floats in water, a glass of water, a paper clip, a small piece of clay, a towel.

1. Find a packet that floats in glass of water, and is narrow enough to fold through the mouth of your soda bottle.

2. Add weight with a paper clip and clay until it almost sinks.

3. Can you make it dive and hover without a lid on your bottle?

Sauce

---

a. Does the condiment packet contain air? How do you know?

b. You want the packet to hover lower in the open air-bottle. What easy adjustment can you make?

TEACHING NOTES

Learning Objective

To invent a Cartesian diver out of unusual materials. To have fun.

Lab Notes

1. We find that salsa packets from Taco Bell® currently support a paper clip plus clay ball. Brands less buoyant than "one paperclip" can be weighted with a staple or pin, plus a small pinch of clay.

Challenge Check-Off

Students should be able to make their divers dive, float, and hover by changing hand pressure on the bottle.

Response Check-Off

a. Yes, the condiment packet must contains air (or some compressible gas). If the packet contained only liquid, it would not expand and contract significantly with changes in pressure, and thus be incapable of displacing more or less water.

b. To make the diver hover lower, remove a bit of clay. This increases its buoyancy, enabling it to hover at greater depths (under more water pressure), regaining the average density of water (the medium that buoys it up).

Test for Understanding

Yesterday your condiment diver floated, sank and hovered. Today it only sinks. What variables may have changed? *It may be experiencing a loss of buoyancy due to increased atmospheric pressure or reduced temperature. Both variables decrease its internal air volume, and thus reduce the weight of water it displaces.*

Going further

Can you find a condiment packet with negative buoyancy and turn it into a diver? *Students might strap on a mini Styrofoam "flotation device" with a rubber band. Or they might squeeze and cap the bottle, before again releasing the bottle. Water will sag inside against the caved-in walls of the container and press them outward. This expands air inside the condiment packet, possibly enough to make it float.*

Challenge: What else makes you curious?

You need: various common materials. These will become apparent as you plan your experiment(s).

N1. Will a diver still dive in a bottle just half full of water?

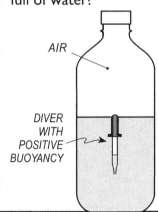

AIR

DIVER WITH POSITIVE BUOYANCY

N2. Can you affect a diver's hover point with a straw "jacket?" A staple "collar?" Other materials?

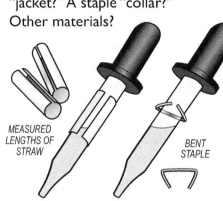

MEASURED LENGTHS OF STRAW

BENT STAPLE

N3. Can you synchronize two divers in one bottle?

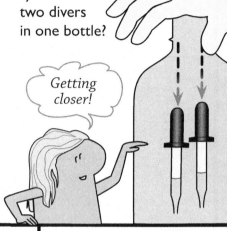

Getting closer!

N4. Can you build a diver out of other materials?

A SECTION OF STRAW, A RUBBER BAND, AND CLAY WILL WORK!

N5. Investigate a test tube diver weighted with paper clips. Does its buoyancy change over time?

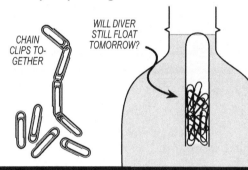

CHAIN CLIPS TOGETHER

WILL DIVER STILL FLOAT TOMORROW?

N6. Ask and answer your own question!

Ⓐ© 2008 by TOPS Learning Systems, Willows, CA 95988. Reproduction limited to personal teaching use by purchaser only. All others please purchase your own copy from www.topscience.org. Thank you!

TEACHING NOTES

Learning Objective

To do science: wonder, predict, experiment, observe, conclude, then ask more questions.

Lab Notes

N1. This diver still works, but with "mushy" squeezes: You have to compress a large volume of air outside the diver to also compress a small volume of air inside it.

N2. Plastic floats on water: This adds buoyancy, so the diver hovers lower. Each 2.5 cm (1 inch) of straw lowers the hover point about 4 cm.

Metal sinks in water: This decreases buoyancy, raising the diver's hover point. A single staple raises the hover point perhaps 14 cm.

N3. It is easy to make a pair of eye droppers sink and float in the same bottle. But they require very fine air-volume adjustments to fall and rise together.

N4. Here is one possible design using a section of a plastic drinking straw, a small rubber band, and clay plugs.

N5. Students should link the clips together. Then bunch this chain inside the mouth of the tube – not too tightly and not too deeply – so friction holds them in place.

It is easy to "knock the wind" out of these divers with a sharp blow to the side of the bottle: Air at the mouth of the test tube bubbles out, and the diver immediately sinks.

Adjust the diver within 1 or 2 paper clip of sinking. Return a few hours later (or the next day), and the diver will always be sunk! Why? Iron paper clips are combining with gaseous oxygen to make solid rust, thus reducing air volume in the tube.

N6. Possible investigations: submarines • hot air balloons • Archimedes and the king's golden crown • swim bladders in fish • scuba diving • Boyle's law • Charles' law • How much does air weigh? • Why do helium balloons rise? • Can you invent a "diving" diver that rescues a "sunken" diver?

Student Notes and Information

✱ How an eyedropper works:

The volume of <u>air</u> that gets squeezed into a container of water...

...equals the volume of <u>water</u> that gets sucked back into the eyedropper when you release the bulb.

✱ **Displacement**: The volume of water pushed aside when you immerse an object.

✱ **Buoyancy**: An upward push on objects immersed in liquid.

Why do I **weigh less in water** than in air?

(Because I am buoyed up by the weight of water I displace.)

A clever ancient Greek named Archimedes explained **buoyancy and displacement** this way:

Archimedes' Principle:

An immersed body is buoyed up with a force equal to the weight of the water it displaces.

Water inside an eyedropper, that has weight in air, weighs nothing in water! Why?

AIR

"weighty" water in air

IN AIR, this water is buoyed up by the weight of <u>air</u> it displaces, which is hardly any weight at all.

IN WATER, this water is buoyed up by the weight of <u>water</u> it displaces, which supports its weight exactly.

WATER

"weightless" water in water

✱ **Eyedropper Questions:**

(1) Which dropper holds more air?
(2) Which dropper holds less water?
(3) Which dropper is weighed down by water?
(4) Which dropper displaces less water?
(5) Which dropper has less buoyancy?
(6) Which dropper displaces more than its weight in water?
(7) Which dropper displaces less than its weight in water?

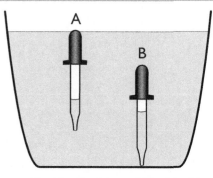

(1) A, (2) A, (3) neither, (4) B, (5) B (6) A, (7) B.

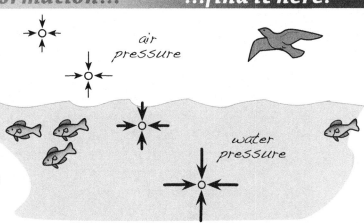

✱ We live under a thick, heavy blanket of air (Earth's atmosphere) that presses equally in all directions, with a force that increases with depth.

Air presses on water, so water also transmits this "pressing" (pressure) in all directions, with a force that increases with depth.

Compressibility: Gases have much more space between their molecules than liquids do. If you squeeze both air and water, only the air will compress to a significantly smaller **volume**.

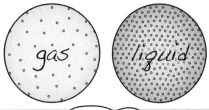

Volume: How much space a substance takes up.

DIVER'S MASS:

AIR

WATER DROPS

(Not part of diver)

Mass: The quantity of matter (amount of "stuff") a body contains. The *total mass* of an eyedropper diver includes the glass, rubber, internal air, plus any water drops clinging *above* the water line. (Water the diver floats in—which can enter and leave the bottom opening—is *not* part of the diver.)

Liquid has greater density than gas.

Density: How much **mass** a substance contains per unit **volume**; a measure of compactness. Objects less dense than water float in water. Objects more dense than water sink in water. Objects with the same density as water (1 g/mL) hover in between.

✱ There are **three** states of buoyancy:

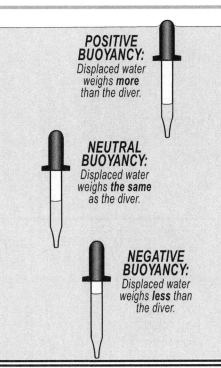

POSITIVE BUOYANCY:
*Displaced water weighs **more** than the diver.*

NEUTRAL BUOYANCY:
*Displaced water weighs **the same** as the diver.*

NEGATIVE BUOYANCY:
*Displaced water weighs **less** than the diver.*

✱ **Newton's Third Law:**
For every action there is an equal and opposite reaction. So while combusting gases are escaping downward from the tail of a rocket (action), the gas is also pushing the rocket upward (reaction) with equal force.

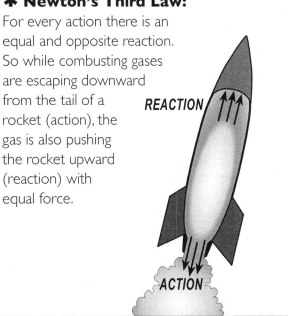

REACTION

ACTION

Diving into Pressure and Buoyancy

✱ **Pressure** in any fluid increases with depth.

✱ Imagine hovering **weightless**, 5 feet under the water. Your weight belt, plus the air you are holding in your lungs and mouth, give you **the same average density as water.**

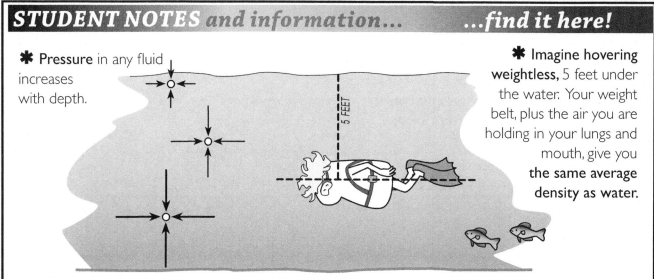

5 FEET

QUESTIONS:

If someone hands you a small rock, will you need to move a little up or down to maintain weightlessness?

(Up. Because the rock increases my average density, I can lower it again by placing myself under less water—causing the air in my mouth and lungs to be less compressed.)

If someone hands you a small air-filled balloon, will you move a little up or down to again hover weightless?

(Down. Because the balloon decreases my average density, I can raise it again by putting myself under more water -- causing the air in my mouth, lungs and balloon to be more compressed.)

If a clear, high pressure weather system moves in, will your hover point remain at exactly 5 feet?

(No, my new hover point will rise to less than 5 feet. Because high air pressure increases my average density, I can lower it again by placing myself under less water -- causing the air in my mouth and lungs to be less compressed.)

✱ **Cohesion** happens when particles of the *same* substance stick together.

Water is strongly *cohesive* because its molecules tend to stick to each other, creating a strong, skin-like surface tension that pulls water drops into round spheres.

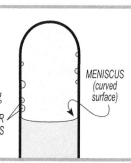

MENISCUS (curved surface)

WATER DROPS

✱ **Adhesion** happens when particles of *different* substances stick together.

Because water and glass are strongly *adhesive*, a meniscus forms in test tubes where water meets glass.

✱ As the **PRESSURE** on a gas **doubles**, its **VOLUME** ideally **halves**.

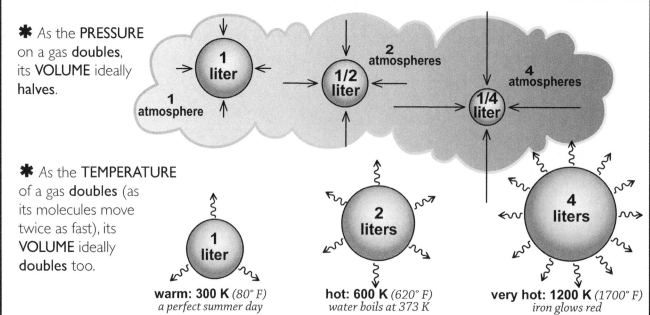

1 liter — 1 atmosphere

1/2 liter — 2 atmospheres

1/4 liter — 4 atmospheres

✱ As the **TEMPERATURE** of a gas **doubles** (as its molecules move twice as fast), its **VOLUME** ideally **doubles** too.

1 liter
warm: 300 K *(80° F)*
a perfect summer day

2 liters
hot: 600 K *(620° F)*
water boils at 373 K

4 liters
very hot: 1200 K *(1700° F)*
iron glows red

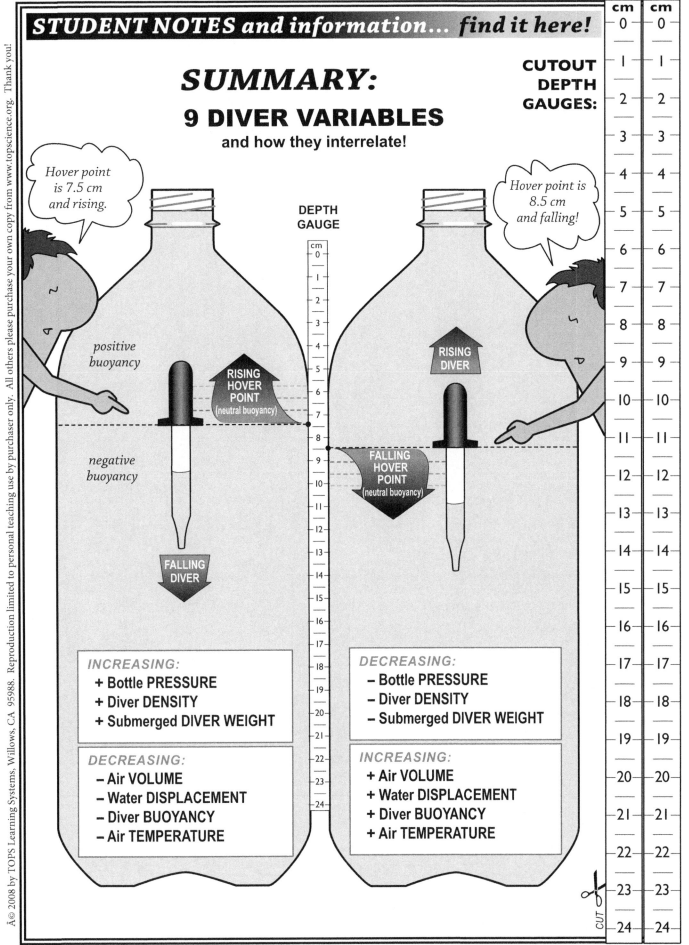

Feedback

If you enjoyed teaching TOPS please tell us so. Your praise motivates us to work hard. If you found an error or can suggest ways to improve this module, we need to hear about that too. Your criticism will help us improve our next new edition. Would you like information about our other publications? Ask us to send you our latest catalog free of charge.

For whatever reason, we'd love to hear from you. We include this self-mailer for your convenience.

Sincerely,

Ron and Peg Marson
author and illustrator

Your Message Here:

Module Title _____ Date _____

Name _____ School _____

Address _____

City _____ State _____ Zip _____

―――――――――――――――――― FIRST FOLD ――――――――――――――――――

―――――――――――――――――― SECOND FOLD ――――――――――――――――――

RETURN ADDRESS

―――――――――――――――――――――――――――――――

―――――――――――――――――――――――――――

―――――――――――――――――――――――――――――――

TOPS Learning Systems
342 S Plumas St
Willows, CA 95988

TAPE HERE